MCR

No Backbone!
The World of Invertebrates

Prickly Sea Stars

by Natalie Lunis

Consultant: Bill Murphy
Marine Biologist, Northern Waters Gallery
New England Aquarium
Boston, MA

BEARPORT
PUBLISHING

NEW YORK, NEW YORK

Credits

Cover and TOC, © seldomsee/istockphoto.com, © Vasile Tiple/istockphoto, © Robert Glusic/Corbis, and © Robin Chittenden/FLPA/
Alamy; Title Page © Robert Glusic/Corbis, and © Robin Chittenden/FLPA/Alamy; 4–5, © age fotostock/SuperStock; 6T, © Comstock
Images/Alamy; 6M, © Jez Tryner 2004/Image Quest Marine; 6B, © Arco/P. Sutter/imagebroker/Alamy; 7, © Darrell Gulin/Corbis;
8, © Sanamyan/Alamy; 10, © Jeff Rotman; 11, © Marilyn Kazmers/Peter Arnold; 12, © Nancy Rotenberg/Animals Animals-Earth
Scenes; 13, © HerbSegars-www.gotosnapshot.com; 14, © Mark Chappell/Animals Animals-Earth Scenes; 15, © Kennan Ward/Corbis;
16–17, © Ingram Publishing/SuperStock; 19, © Doug Perrine/NaturePL; 20, © Enrico Caracciolo/CuboImages srl/Alamy; 21, © Steve
Simonsen; 22TL, © SUNNYphotography.com/Alamy; 22TR, © Jane Burton/Bruce Coleman Inc./Alamy; 22BL, © Mike Kelly/The Image
Bank/Getty Images; 22BR, © Norbert Wu/Minden Pictures; 22 Spot, © pixelman/Shutterstock; 23TL, © Jim Wehtje/Photodisc Green/
Getty Images; 23TR, © Sanamyan/Alamy; 23BL, © Darrell Gulin/Corbis; 23BR, © Andrew J. Martinez/SeaPics.

Publisher: Kenn Goin
Editorial Director: Adam Siegel
Creative Director: Spencer Brinker
Design: Dawn Beard Creative
Photo Researcher: James O'Connor

Library of Congress Cataloging-in-Publication Data

Lunis, Natalie.
  Prickly sea stars / by Natalie Lunis.
     p. cm. — (No backbone! : the world of invertebrates)
  Includes bibliographical references and index.
  ISBN-13: 978-1-59716-508-2 (lib. bdg.)
  ISBN-10: 1-59716-508-5 (lib. bdg.)
  1. Starfishes—Juvenile literature. I. Title.

  QL384.A8L86 2008
  593.9'3—dc22

                        2007006928

For more information, write to Bearport Publishing Company, Inc., 101 Fifth Avenue, Suite 6R,
New York, New York 10003. Printed in the United States of America.

10 9 8 7 6 5 4 3 2

Contents

Stars of the Sea. 4

Many Kinds, Many Colors 6

Life Without a Brain 8

Sea Food 10

Open for Dinner 12

Prickly Protection 14

Regrowing a Ray 16

More Ways to Grow. 18

A Story of Survival 20

A World of Invertebrates 22

Glossary 23

Index. 24

Read More. 24

Learn More Online. 24

Stars of the Sea

Sea stars are animals that live in the sea.

Some people call them starfish, but they are not fish.

All fish have **backbones**.

backbone

Sea stars don't have backbones.

They don't even have heads!

A sea star gets its name from the way its body is shaped—like a star.

Many Kinds, Many Colors

There are about 1,800 kinds of sea stars.

Some sea stars are as small as one inch (2.5 cm) across.

Others are as big as two feet (61 cm).

Sea stars can be many different colors.

Yet they all have arms, called **rays**, connected to the center of their bodies.

Most sea stars have five rays, but some have up to 40.

Life Without a Brain

Sea stars don't have a head or a brain.

Yet they can still sense the world around them.

They use tiny body parts called **eyespots** to see light and dark.

They use parts of their skin to smell other sea creatures.

A sea star's eyespots are on the tips of its rays.

Sea Food

Some sea stars use their sense of smell to hunt for food.

They can smell clams, mussels, snails, and other small sea creatures.

The sea stars slowly crawl toward the animals and grab them.

Sea stars have many little **tube feet** on the underside of their rays. The tube feet help them crawl and grab on to things.

tube feet

clam

Open for Dinner

Sea stars eat clams and mussels in a strange way.

They grab the shells with their tube feet.

They pull until the shells open up just a little.

Then the sea stars push out their stomachs through their mouths.

They squeeze their stomachs into the shells and eat the animals inside.

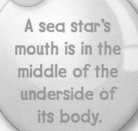

A sea star's mouth is in the middle of the underside of its body.

Prickly Protection

Few animals hunt sea stars for food. Why?

Most sea stars have bodies that are covered with prickly skin.

The prickly skin makes them hard to eat.

Some fish and crabs are able to eat sea stars, though.

Seagulls and otters sometimes catch and eat them, too.

A few kinds of sea stars are not prickly. Instead, they are slimy or leathery.

sea otter

Regrowing a Ray

A sea star sometimes loses a ray in a struggle with an enemy.

When this happens, it grows a new ray.

For a while, the new ray is smaller than the others.

In a few months, it grows to full size.

A sea star can also lose a ray if it is crushed by a rock or other heavy object.

new ray

17

More Ways to Grow

Sea stars can grow back more than just one ray.

They can grow back two, three, four, or even more rays.

Sometimes one chopped-off ray can grow into a whole new sea star!

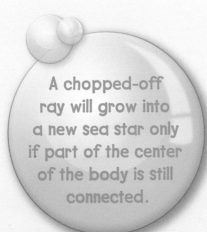

A chopped-off ray will grow into a new sea star only if part of the center of the body is still connected.

A Story of Survival

For a long time, people have caught clams and oysters for food.

In the past, they would chop up any sea stars they found in their nets.

Then they would throw them back into the sea.

The people thought they were getting rid of the sea stars.

In fact, they were causing even more sea stars to grow!

Sea stars live in all the world's oceans. They live in warm, cold, shallow, and deep waters.

A World of Invertebrates

Animals that have backbones are known as *vertebrates* (VUR-tuh-brits). Mammals, birds, fish, reptiles, and amphibians are all vertebrates.

Animals that don't have backbones are *invertebrates* (in-VUR-tuh-brits). Worms, jellyfish, snails, and sea stars are all invertebrates. So are all insects and spiders. More than 95 percent of all kinds of animals are invertebrates.

Here are four invertebrates that are closely related to sea stars. Like sea stars, they all live in the ocean.

Sea Urchin

Sea Cucumber

Brittle Star

Sand Dollars

Glossary

backbones
(BAK-*bohnz*)
a group of
connected bones
that run along
the backs of some
animals, such as
dogs, cats, and fish;
also called spines

eyespots
(EYE-spots)
parts of a sea
star's body that
can sense light
and dark

rays (RAYZ)
arm-like body
parts that grow
from the center
of a sea star's
body

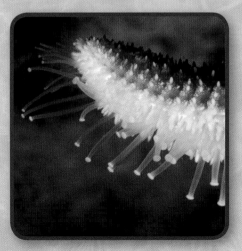

tube feet
(TOOB FEET)
small body
parts that are
attached to a
sea star's rays
and help it
crawl

Index

backbones 4, 22

brittle star 22

colors 6

eating 12

enemies 14–15, 16

eyespots 8–9

fish 4, 14, 22

food 10, 12, 14, 20

hunting 10, 14

mouths 12

rays 6, 9, 10, 16–17, 18–19

sand dollars 22

sea cucumber 22

sea urchin 22

senses 8, 10

size 6

skin 8, 14

stomachs 12–13

tube feet 10, 12

Read More

Stone, Lynn M. *Sea Stars*. Vero Beach, FL: Rourke Publishing (2006).

Svancara, Theresa. *Sea Stars and Other Echinoderms*. Chicago: World Book, Inc. (2002).

Zuchora-Walske, Christine. *Spiny Sea Stars*. Minneapolis, MN: Lerner (2001).

Learn More Online

To learn more about sea stars, visit **www.bearportpublishing.com/NoBackbone**